THE
Wedding Planner
CHECKLIST

A PORTABLE GUIDE TO ORGANIZING
YOUR DREAM WEDDING

PETER PAUPER PRESS, INC.
WHITE PLAINS, NEW YORK

PETER PAUPER PRESS
Fine Books and Gifts Since 1928

Our Company

In 1928, at the age of twenty-two, Peter Beilenson began printing books on a small press in the basement of his parents' home in Larchmont, New York. Peter—and later, his wife, Edna—sought to create fine books that sold at "prices even a pauper could afford."

Today, still family owned and operated, Peter Pauper Press continues to honor our founders' legacy—and our customers' expectations—of beauty, quality, and value.

WRITTEN BY JAX BERMAN AND ADAPTED FROM *MY WEDDING PLANNER*
BY SARA MILLER AND KAREN BERMAN

ILLUSTRATIONS COPYRIGHT © MARUSHABELLE,
USED UNDER LICENSE FROM SHUTTERSTOCK.COM

DESIGNED BY MARGARET RUBIANO

VISIT US AT WWW.PETERPAUPER.COM

TABLE OF CONTENTS

∽⊙ INTRODUCTION ⊙∼

ALTHOUGH A WEDDING IS A JOYOUS OCCASION, PLANNING one can be a stressful and time-consuming experience. You're constantly on the go and juggling incredible amounts of information all at once. This planner will help make organizing your big day a little easier by giving you a portable space to jot down your thoughts. Keep this book in your purse or bag so it will always be within reach as you visit dressmakers, bakeries, florists, venues, and more.

Within these pages, you'll find checklists and charts to keep track of information you'll acquire as you meet with the various people who will help to make your big day a one-of-a-kind occasion that's just right for you. It is, in other words, for on-the-go note-taking. For a more in-depth overview of your wedding, we recommend using a notebook alongside this planner to capture the ideas that you'll be developing as you sit down and devote time to your vision. The notes you take via this pocket-sized planner can be your jumping-off point to the bigger picture. This planner also includes a handy inside back cover pocket for business cards and magazine clippings as well as tips scattered throughout to help you further develop your ideas.

Most of all, have fun! This is your chance to make your dreams become reality, so let yourself dream big.

• YOUR BASICS •

DATE/TIME .... LOCATION ....

....

COLORS ....

THEME ....

....

IMPORTANT NAMES AND NUMBERS

Wedding planner/consultant ....

Dressmaker ....

Tailor ....

Ceremony venue ....

Reception venue ....

Officiant ....

Band leader/musicians—ceremony ....

Band leader/musicians—reception ....

DJ ....

Caterer ....

Liquor services ....

Florist ....

Photographer ....

Videographer ....

Stationer ....

Baker ....

Decorations ....

Favors ....

Rentals & supplies ....

Rehearsal dinner venue ....

Transportation company ....

TIMELINE

TWELVE TO SIX MONTHS BEFORE THE WEDDING

- ○ Hold engagement party
- ○ Decide whether or not you want a wedding consultant or planner. Interview different candidates and select one. (NOTE: If planning a destination wedding in a foreign country, this is essential!)
- ○ Select date
- ○ Set budget and establish priorities
- ○ If planning a destination wedding, research destinations and book early
- ○ Reserve wedding and reception sites; confirm date and times
- ○ Make sure venue is kid-friendly if children are attending
- ○ Consider insurance for your venue in case of illness or bad weather
- ○ Choose a caterer; include your DJ, photographer, etc., in your plate count
- ○ Compile guest list
- ○ Choose and retain officiant
- ○ Choose and notify attendants
- ○ Order dress and accessories
- ○ Book florist and choose arrangements
- ○ Book photographer (If taking photos in a park, etc., check to see if you need a permit. Have a backup plan in the event of a weather-related disruption of outdoor photo shoot.)
- ○ Book videographer
- ○ Book a band or DJ for the reception
- ○ Book musicians for the ceremony
- ○ Plan and book your honeymoon
- ○ Find out when final payments for everything are due

PRO TIP: Planning a destination wedding in an exotic location? There are wedding consultants dedicated to doing all the legwork for you, including booking hotel rooms and more. However, for a local wedding, book hotel rooms within a reasonable time frame, according to what your town is like. New Yorkers who want cosmopolitan summer weddings may need to book several months in advance, whereas country brides in much smaller towns may get away with booking much closer to their wedding date.

SIX TO FOUR MONTHS BEFORE THE WEDDING

- ◯ Reserve rental equipment
- ◯ Register for gifts
- ◯ Order wedding cake
- ◯ Select stationery, including thank you cards
- ◯ Purchase or reserve groom's attire
- ◯ Select wedding rings
- ◯ Choose favors
- ◯ Choose gifts for wedding party and groom
- ◯ Reserve room for wedding night
- ◯ Arrange transportation

FOUR TO TWO MONTHS BEFORE THE WEDDING

- ◯ Discuss details of menu with caterer
- ◯ Discuss service with officiant
- ◯ Choose readings for the ceremony
- ◯ Schedule rehearsal time and rehearsal dinner

TWO MONTHS TO ONE MONTH BEFORE THE WEDDING

- ◯ Purchase guest book
- ◯ Have programs printed
- ◯ Mail invitations
- ◯ Send list of accommodations to out-of-town guests
- ◯ Complete proper documents for name change, if desired
- ◯ Send change-of-address information to post office
- ◯ Have makeup artist and hairstylist do a trial run
- ◯ Obtain marriage license
- ◯ Attend and write thank you notes for bridal shower

THREE WEEKS BEFORE THE WEDDING

- ◯ Confirm hotel and transportation reservations for out-of-town guests
- ◯ Finalize song list for band or DJ

TWO WEEKS BEFORE THE WEDDING

- ○ Have final dress fitting (Practice with shoes!)
- ○ Arrange seating plan and write place cards
- ○ Notify caterer of final guest count
- ○ Attend and write thank you notes for bachelor/bachelorette party

ONE WEEK BEFORE THE WEDDING

- ○ Pick up dress or have it delivered
- ○ Begin writing thank yous for gifts that have arrived by mail
- ○ Pack for honeymoon
- ○ Confirm travel arrangements
- ○ Confirm details with caterer
- ○ Hold the bridal luncheon

ONE DAY BEFORE THE WEDDING

- ○ Finalize seating chart
- ○ Confirm limousines or other transportation
- ○ Give any thank you cards you've already written to maid of honor to mail after the wedding
- ○ Have manicure and pedicure
- ○ Give gift to each member of the wedding party
- ○ Rehearsal ceremony and dinner

THE WEDDING DAY

- ○ Run through order of events in your mind
- ○ Have a little something to eat
- ○ Hair and makeup
- ○ Relax and enjoy your day!

PRO TIP: If your wedding party is planning your bridal shower or bachelorette party, that doesn't mean you don't have to worry about them! Your honor attendant will most likely keep you informed of the time and theme of your shower and party. Plan accordingly!

∽ BUDGETING ∾

BRIDAL ATTIRE		
	BUDGETED COST	ACTUAL COST
Dress		
Alterations		
Headpiece and veil		
Undergarments		
Shoes		
Jewelry		
Hair		
Makeup		
Nails		
Other		
Total		

BRIDAL ATTENDANTS' ATTIRE		
	BUDGETED COST	ACTUAL COST
Honor Attendant's Attire		
Alterations		
Bridal Attendants' Attire		
Alterations		
Shoes		
Accessories		
Other		
Total		

GROOM'S ATTIRE		
	BUDGETED COST	ACTUAL COST
Tuxedo/Suit		
Alterations		
Shoes		
Other		
Total		

GROOM'S ATTENDANTS' ATTIRE		
	BUDGETED COST	ACTUAL COST
Honor Attendant's Attire		
Alterations		
Groom's Attendants' Attire		
Alterations		
Shoes		
Other		
Total		

CHILDREN'S ATTIRE		
	BUDGETED COST	ACTUAL COST
Flower Girl's Dress		
Alterations		
Ring Bearer's Attire		
Alterations		
Shoes		
Other		
Total		

STATIONERY		
	BUDGETED COST	ACTUAL COST
Invitations		
Response cards		
Other enclosures		
Table cards		
Place cards		
Programs		
Thank you cards		
Other		
Total		

CEREMONY		
	BUDGETED COST	ACTUAL COST
Ceremony site		
Officiant		
Rental fees		
Other		
Total		

PRO TIP: Your wedding will take months of planning, so you may change your vision frequently and abruptly. Never forget to get everything in writing, even the smallest changes, so your bill at the end of the day doesn't come as a complete shock to you. Don't forget to read your contracts over carefully as well!

RECEPTION		
	BUDGETED COST	ACTUAL COST
Food		
Bar		
Cake		
Service		
Rental fees		
Gratuities		
Parking		
Coat check		
Tax		
Other		
Total		

MUSIC		
	BUDGETED COST	ACTUAL COST
Ceremony		
Reception		
Other		
Total		

PHOTOGRAPHY		
	BUDGETED COST	ACTUAL COST
Engagement portraits		
Wedding portraits		
Photographer		
Wedding album		
Parents' albums		
Videography		
Other		
Total		

FLOWERS		
	BUDGETED COST	ACTUAL COST
Ceremony		
Bride's bouquet		
Bridesmaids' bouquets		
Children's flowers		
Corsages		
Boutonnieres		
Centerpieces		
Other		
Total		

PARTIES		
	BUDGETED COST	ACTUAL COST
ENGAGEMENT PARTY		
Venue		
Food		
Drink		
REHEARSAL DINNER		
Venue		
Food		
Drink		
POST-WEDDING BRUNCH		
Venue		
Food		
Drink		
Other		
Total		

HONEYMOON		
	BUDGETED COST	ACTUAL COST
Airfare		
Hotel		
Transportation		
Other		
Total		

MISCELLANEOUS		
	BUDGETED COST	ACTUAL COST
Marriage license		
Bride's wedding ring		
Groom's wedding ring		
Transportation		
For the bridal party		
For guests		
Favors		
Flower girls' baskets		
Ring pillow		
Guest book		
Other		
Total		

	BUDGETED COST	ACTUAL COST
TOTAL		

PRO TIP: Give your honor attendant envelopes containing checks and tips for your servers, your caterers, your bar, and so forth before the event, and have them collect checks from guests and store them in a safe place. It's your attendant's duty to worry about your finances on the big day, not yours!

PARTIES

THE ENGAGEMENT PARTY

Venue

Location

Host

Date/Time

Address

Website

Phone

Email

Food & Drinks

Caterer

Contact

Address/Website

Phone

Email

Menu

Drinks

THE REHEARSAL DINNER

Venue

Location

Host

Date/Time

Address

Website

Phone

Email

Food & Drinks

Caterer

Contact

Address

Website

Phone

Email

Menu

Drinks

Venue

Location

Host

Date/Time

Address/Website

Phone/Email

Food & Drinks

Caterer

Contact

Address

Website

Phone

Email

Menu

Drinks

BRIDAL SHOWER/BACHELORETTE PARTY CHECKLIST

Date/time of bridal shower ....

Held by ....

Location ....

Date/time of bachelorette party ....

Held by ....

Location ....

	BRIDAL SHOWER	BACHELORETTE PARTY
Communicate with honor attendant about date	○	○
Obtain outfit (if party is themed)	○	○
Cost	○ _____	○ _____
Arrange for transportation to/from party	○	○
Cost	○ _____	○ _____
Take note of each guest and which gift they gave	○	○
Write thank you notes to each guest	○	○

GIFT REGISTRY

STORE

Address ....

Email ....

Website ....

Login .... Password ....

STORE

Address ....

Email ....

Website ....

Login .... Password ....

STORE

Address ....

Email ....

Website ....

Login .... Password ....

STORE

Address ....

Email ....

Website ....

Login .... Password ....

ATTIRE, HAIR, AND MAKEUP

Purchased from ....

Salesperson ....

Address/Website ....

Phone/Email ....

Designer .... Size ....

Color .... Style ....

Fitting Schedule

First fitting date .... Time ....

Second fitting date .... Time ....

Final fitting date .... Time ....

Date dress will be ready ....

Picked up/Delivered? ....

PRO TIP: Although you may be tempted to bring an entire party with you to show off your wedding gown, only bring one or two people whose opinions matter most to you. Any more than that, and you'll be overwhelmed by the plethora of opinions!

	Accessory 1	Accessory 2	Accessory 3
Accessory			
Purchased from			
Salesperson			
Address/Website			
Phone/Email			
Designer/Size			
Color/Style			
Cost			
Date item will be ready			
Picked up/Delivered?			

	Accessory 4	Accessory 5	Accessory 6
Accessory			
Purchased from			
Salesperson			
Address/Website			
Phone/Email			
Designer/Size			
Color/Style			
Cost			
Date item will be ready			
Picked up/Delivered?			

PRO TIP: Remember to bring your hair decorations—veil, tiara, flowers, and so forth—so your stylist can design around them!

	WEDDING SHOES	HOSIERY/UNDERWEAR
Purchased from		
Salesperson		
Address/Website		
Phone/Email		
Designer		
Size		
Color		
Style		
Date ready		
Picked up/Delivered?		

BEAUTY SERVICES

	HAIR	FACE	MANICURE	PEDICURE
Salon				
Address/Website				
Phone/Email				
Stylist/Artist				
Date/Time				

Color/design of makeup and nails:

....

....

OTHER SERVICES	
Type of Service	
Salon	
Address/Website	
Phone/Email	
Date/Time	

WEDDING RINGS

Purchased from ....

Salesperson ....

Address/Website ....

Phone/Email ....

Description of bride's ring ....

Size ....

Engraving ....

Description of groom's ring ....

Size ....

Engraving ....

Date rings will be ready ....

Picked up/Delivered? ....

OTHER WEDDING JEWELRY			
	PIECE 1	PIECE 2	PIECE 3
Piece			
Purchased from			
Salesperson			
Address/Website			
Phone/Email			
Designer/Size			
Color/Style			
Cost			
Date item will be ready			
Picked up/Delivered?			

BRIDAL ATTENDANTS' ATTIRE

Honor Attendant's Dress

Purchased from ....

Salesperson ....

Address/Website ....

Phone/Email ....

Designer ....

Color .... Style ....

Date ready ....

Picked up/Delivered? ....

Bridal Attendants' Dresses

Purchased from ....

Salesperson ....

Address/Website ....

Phone/Email ....

Designer ....

Color .... Style ....

Date ready ....

Picked up/Delivered? ....

Shoes

Purchased from ....

Salesperson ....

Address/Website ....

Phone/Email ....

Designer ....

Color .... Style ....

Date ready ....

Picked up/Delivered? ....

ATTENDANT'S NAME	CLOTHING SIZE	SHOE SIZE

ACCESSORIES			
Accessory			
Purchased from			
Salesperson			
Address/Website			
Phone			
Email			
Designer			
Color			
Style			
Date ready			
Picked up/Delivered?			

GROOM'S ATTIRE

Apparel

Description ....

Purchased/rented from ....

Salesperson ....

Address/Website ....

Phone/Email ....

Designer .... Size ....

Color .... Style ....

Fitting Schedule

First fitting date..Time...

Second fitting date..Time...

Final fitting date..Time...

OTHER ATTIRE/ACCESSORIES		
Accessory		
Purchased from		
Salesperson		
Address/Website		
Phone/Email		
Designer		
Color		
Style		
Date item will be ready		
Picked up/Delivered?		

GROOM'S ATTENDANTS' ATTIRE

Apparel

Description ....

Purchased/rented from ....

Salesperson ....

Address/Website ....

Phone/Email ....

Designer .... Size ....

Color .... Style ....

Picked up/Delivered? ....

Accessory

Item ....

Purchased/rented from ....

Salesperson ....

Address/Website ....

Phone/Email ....

Designer .... Size ....

Color .... Style ....

Picked up/Delivered? ....

ATTENDANT'S NAME	CLOTHING SIZE	SHOE SIZE

CHILDREN'S ATTIRE

Flower Girl's Dress

Purchased from .... Salesperson ....

Address/Website ....

Phone/Email ....

Designer ....

Color .... Style ....

Date ready .... Picked up? .... Sent? ....

FLOWER GIRL'S NAME	CLOTHING SIZE	SHOE SIZE

Ring Bearer's Apparel

Description ....

Purchased from .... Salesperson ....

Address/Website ....

Phone/Email ....

Designer ....

Color .... Style ....

Date ready .... Picked up? .... Sent? ....

RING BEARER'S NAME	CLOTHING SIZE	SHOE SIZE

ACCOMMODATIONS, TRANSPORTATION, AND ACTIVITIES

Bride Before the Wedding

Hotel ....

Address/Website ....

Phone/Email ....

Room .... Rate ....

Check-in day and time .... Check-out day and time ....

Other services (massage, champagne breakfast, etc.) ....

....

....

Groom Before the Wedding

Hotel ....

Address/Website ....

Phone/Email ....

Room .... Rate ....

Check-in day and time .... Check-out day and time ....

Other services (massage, champagne breakfast, etc.) ....

....

....

The Married Couple After the Wedding

Hotel ....

Address/Website ....

Phone/Email ....

Room .... Rate ....

Check-in day and time .... Check-out day and time ....

Other services (massage, champagne breakfast, etc.) ....

The Wedding Party

Hotel ....

Address/Website ....

Phone/Email ....

Room .... Rate ....

Check-in time .... Check-out time ....

Other services (massage, champagne breakfast, etc.) ....

NAME	ROOM	ARRIVE	DEPART

Out-Of-Town Guests

Hotel ....

Address/Website ....

Phone/Email ....

Block of rooms reserved? ....Room rate...........................

Check-in time ....Check-out time...........................

Other services (massage, champagne breakfast, etc.)..

....

....

....

....

NAME	ROOM	ARRIVE	DEPART

NAME	ROOM	ARRIVE	DEPART

PRO TIP: Many hotels will allow you to reserve blocks of rooms for group rates. Taking advantage of this is a great way to cut down on costs and headaches for both you and your wedding guests.

TRANSPORTATION

Transportation for the Wedding Party

Transportation service ....

Address/Website ....

Phone/Email ....

Type of vehicle(s) .... Number of vehicles ....

NAME	PICKUP PLACE	PICKUP TIME

Transportation for Out-of-Town Guests

Transportation service ....

Address/Website ....

Phone/Email ....

Type of vehicle(s) .... Number of vehicles .... Number of guests ....

NAME	PICKUP PLACE	PICKUP TIME

ACTIVITIES FOR OUT-OF-TOWN GUESTS

Restaurants

_____

_____

_____

_____

_____

Places of Interest

_____

_____

_____

_____

Babysitters

_____

_____

_____

_____

~ STATIONERY ~

Contact person ....

Address/Website ....

Phone/Email ....

Description ....

Date stationery will be ready .... Picked up? .... Sent? ....

	ITEM	QUANTITY ORDERED	COST
Save-the-Dates			
Invitation			
Response cards			
Other enclosures			
Announcements			
Programs			
Place cards			
Note cards			
Favor tags			
Maps			
Other			

PRO TIP: As tempting as it is to do an evite, etiquette states formal weddings should avoid going paperless to make the tone of the event clear to guests. However, for casual weddings, evites can be a fun yet practical way to show off the wedding couple's style *and* to save money.

WORDING OF INVITATION

_____

_____

_____

_____

_____

_____

_____

_____

_____

RESPONSE CARD WORDING

_____

_____

_____

_____

OTHER

_____

_____

_____

_____

FLOWERS

Contact ....

Address/Website ....

Phone/Email ....

Date and time of delivery ....

BOUQUETS

For the Bride

Description ....

....

....

....

....

....

For the Bridesmaids

Description ....

....

....

....

For the Flower Girl(s)

Description ....

....

....

For the Mother of the Bride

Description ....

....

....

For the Mother of the Groom

Description ....

....

....

Other

Description ....

....

BOUTONNIERES

For the Groom

Description ....

....

....

For the Groomsmen

Description ....

....

....

For the Father of the Bride

Description ....

....

....

For the Father of the Groom

Description ....

....

For the Ring Bearer

Description ....

....

....

Other

Description ....

....

FLOWERS FOR THE CEREMONY SITE

Description ....

....

....

....

....

FLOWERS FOR THE RECEPTION

Table arrangements ....

....

....

....

Additional flowers for the reception site ....

....

....

....

ADDITIONAL DECORATIONS				
ITEM	QTY	COLOR	# ORDERED/ RENTED	DELIVERED?
Table linen				
Ring pillow				
Tea lights				
String lights/lanterns				
Other candles				
Garlands				
Aisle runners				
Rice/petals/etc.				
Arches				
Canopy/chuppah/mandap				
Chair covers				
Cake topper				
Card box/wishing well				
Other:				

PRO TIP: When choosing flowers, be aware of when your wedding will take place. Buy seasonally according to your wedding date to get the best prices, and avoid Valentine's Day and Mother's Day to avoid sky-high costs!

MUSIC

Musicians

Contact ....

Phone/Email ....

Address/Website ....

Booked from .... to ....

Prelude and Processional

Prelude ....

Processional ....

Bridal march ....

Ceremony

Hymns ....

....

Other ....

Other ....

Other ....

Recessional

....

....

....

....

Band/DJ

Contact ....

Phone/Email ....

Address/Website ....

Booked from .... to ....

Musical Schedule   *Title of Selection*

First dance ....

Bride's dance with father ....

Groom's dance with mother ....

Cake cutting ....

Throwing the bouquet ....

Last dance ....

Other ....

Other ....

Playlist/Must-have songs ....

....

....

....

....

Additional songs you'd like to hear ....

....

....

PHOTOGRAPHY

PRE-CEREMONY

Informal

Photographer ....

Time photographer arrives ....

Phone/Email ....

Date/Time ....

Additional cost ....

Date photos will be ready .... Picked up? .... Sent? ....

Formal Portraits

Photographer ....

Address/Website ....

Phone/Email ....

Date/Time ....

Sizes and quantities of photos included ....

Additional prints ordered ....

Additional cost ....

Date photos will be ready .... Picked up? .... Sent? ....

ONLINE ALBUM(S)	
Website	
Album details	
Login	
Password	

THE CEREMONY & THE RECEPTION

Photographer .... Assistant ....

Address/Website ....

Phone/Email ....

Photographer booked from .... to ....

B&W .... Color .... Both ....

Sizes and quantities of photos included ....

Additional prints ordered ....

Date photos will be ready .... Picked up? ....Sent? ....

Special instructions ("Don't put X next to Y," etc.)

....

....

....

Videography

Videographer .... Assistant ....

Address/Website ....

Phone/Email ....

Videographer booked from .... to ....

Number of video copies included ....

Date video will be ready .... Picked up? .... Sent? ....

Must-Have Photos

....

....

....

THE CEREMONY

OFFICIANT

Name ....

Address ....

Phone/Email ....

Officiant retained from .... to ....

Paid? ○

VENUE

Name ....

Contact person ....

Address/Website ....

Phone/Email ....

Venue retained from .... to ....

Restrictions ....

Deposit paid? ○

Balance due .... Paid? ○

ITEMS RENTED

Rental company ....

Contact person ....

Address/Website ....

Phone/Email ....

Time and date of delivery ....

Items included ....

Jot down ideas for your vows below:

....

....

....

....

....

....

....

....

....

....

....

....

....

....

....

....

....

....

....

PRO TIP: Ceremony readings don't have to be religious in nature. The main idea is that they capture the bond between you and your partner. Other possible sources for readings include poetry, song lyrics, love letters between historical figures and their partners, novels, plays, movies, inspirational essays, or even children's books. You might also find passages in cultural or spiritual texts other than those of your own background, or look to your family for a wise word or few. Be creative, and choose passages that speak to you!

PRO TIP: The order of the ceremony should be planned in advance so all participants know what to do and when to do it. Be sure to discuss any deviations from "standard" practice with your officiant beforehand. They will guide you as to the best way to incorporate these gestures so that they are meaningful and flow with the service. If you want to go with tradition, services often follow the general outline below.

- THE PROCESSION *Use this space to note the order of the procession.*

- THE OFFICIANT'S REMARKS
- SPECIAL READINGS OR MUSIC

- THE EXCHANGE OF VOWS AND RINGS
- THE PRONOUNCEMENT OF MARRIAGE
- THE RECESSIONAL
- THE RECEIVING LINE *Use this space for noting who stands where.*

THE RECEPTION

THE ORDER OF THE RECEPTION

- COCKTAIL HOUR/PICTURES
- INTRODUCTION OF THE WEDDING PARTY AND NEWLYWEDS
- FIRST DANCE
- CHAMPAGNE TOAST/SPEECHES *Use this space for noting who will be toasting*

  or speaking, in what order. ....

  ....

  ....

  ....

  ....

- DINNER
- SPECIAL DANCES *Father-daughter dance, followed by mother-son dance*
- BOUQUET AND GARTER TOSS
- MORE DANCING
- WEDDING CAKE CUTTING

PRO TIP: Holding the wedding and reception in the same place doesn't just cut down on costs. It also makes navigating from the big event to the after party less of a headache for you and your guests. However, if your customs state that you need to be married by a religious officiant, in a religious establishment, remember to ask about whether or not your officiant can perform weddings anywhere or whether or not you can hold a reception at your religious site.

RECEPTION VENUE

Contact ....

Address/Website ....

Phone/Email ....

Reception site booked from .... to ....

Time available: ....

Restrictions ....

....

Goods and services provided ....

....

....

Goods and services available for additional cost ....

....

....

....

TENT

Tent rental company ....

Contact person ....

Address/Website ....

Phone/Email ....

Tent description ....

Other rented items ....

....

Time and date of delivery ....

LIGHTING

Lighting rental company ....

Contact person ....

Address/Website ....

Phone/Email ....

Lighting description ....

....

Time and date of delivery ....

OTHER RENTALS

Company ....

Contact person ....

Address/Website ....

Phone/Email ....

Description of rental items ....

....

Time and date of delivery ....

Company ....

Contact person ....

Address/Website ....

Phone/Email ....

Description of rental items ....

....

Time and date of delivery ....

CATERING

CATERING COMPANY

Contact person ....

Address/Website ....

Phone/Email ....

Caterer booked from .... to ....

Service booked from .... to ....

Final guest count .... Cost per person ....

Number of servers .... Cost per server ....

Deposit paid ○

Balance due .... Paid ○

Reception Menu

Hors d'oeuvres ....
....

Appetizers ....
....

Entrées ....
....

Accompaniments ....
....

Desserts ....
....

Beverages ....
....

Food Restrictions

Food allergies/sensitivities ....

Vegetarians/vegans ....

Other dietary considerations ....

REFRESHMENTS

Beverage supplier ....

Contact person ....

Address/Website ....

Phone/Email ....

Beverages ordered ....

Time and date of delivery ....

THE WEDDING CAKE

Bakery ....

Contact person ....

Address/Website ....

Phone/Email ....

Wedding cake description ....

Time and date of delivery ....

Deposit paid ○

Balance due .... Paid ○

THE GROOM'S CAKE

Bakery ....

Contact person ....

Address/Website ....

Phone/Email ....

Groom's cake description ....

....

Time and date of delivery ....

Deposit paid ○

Balance due .... Paid ○

WEDDING FAVORS

Store ....

Contact person ....

Address/Website ....

Phone/Email ....

Description of favors ....

....

Quantity ordered ....

Date favors will be ready ....

Picked up? .... Sent? ....

OTHER

_____

_____

_____

_____

_____

_____

_____

_____

_____

_____

_____

_____

_____

_____

_____

PRO TIP: Want a fancy, floral wedding cake? Be warned! Sugar or gum paste flowers are more expensive than fresh ones. For an elegant, springtime look, consider using fresh, edible blossoms for decoration instead, or forgo the cake for other desserts. Cupcake trees, doughnut stands, and macaron towers are all modern, popular ideas that are easier on your wallet than a traditional cake.

HONEYMOON PLANNER

SIX MONTHS OR MORE BEFORE HONEYMOON

- ○ Set budget
- ○ Choose destination
- ○ Reserve airline tickets
- ○ Reserve hotel
- ○ Reserve rental car

THREE MONTHS BEFORE HONEYMOON

- ○ Obtain or renew passports
- ○ Arrange for visas, if necessary
- ○ Finalize reservations

ONE MONTH BEFORE HONEYMOON

- ○ Confirm reservations
- ○ Purchase items for travel

- ○ Book activities that require reservations

TWO WEEKS BEFORE HONEYMOON

- ○ Arrange transportation to and from airports
- ○ Draw cash in country's currency, if going abroad
- ○ Contact bank to inform them of your travel, if going abroad
- ○ Be sure to make copies of your ID. Take a set with you in your luggage, and leave a set at home with a trusted friend or relative.
- ○ Arrange for care of pets

ONE WEEK BEFORE HONEYMOON
- ○ Pack
- ○ Confirm travel arrangements
- ○ Ask post office to hold mail
- ○ Contact gift registry to hold delivery

ONE DAY BEFORE HONEYMOON
- ○ Reconfirm flights
- ○ Give itinerary to a friend or family member in case of emergency

PRO TIP: After months of planning, rest and relaxation is essential for your honeymoon. Keep your stress levels at a minimum by avoiding early-morning flights the day after your wedding. Also, having an open day or two, as opposed to a schedule packed to the brim with sightseeing and traveling, can allow you to take it easy ... or enjoy a little spontaneity.

POST-WEDDING CHECKLIST

WEDDING-RELATED TASKS   DATE DONE

○ Return tuxedos and rented attire   ....

○ Return rented equipment and accessories   ....

○ Have wedding gown professionally dry-cleaned and packaged   ....

○ Preserve bridal bouquet   ....

○ After honeymoon, contact gift registry to restart delivery;
   restart mail and newspapers   ....

○ Review proofs and order photographs   ....

○ Write thank you notes   ....

○ Review your finances with your new spouse   ....

○ Buy life insurance or change beneficiaries   ....

○ Add spouse's name or change beneficiaries for IRAs and other
   financial instruments, both personal and through your job   ....

○ Visit your lawyer to make or update your wills   ....

○ Consult a financial planner   ....

○ Change your name (if you wish to)   ....

○ Send out new contact information or change
   of address (if necessary)   ....

SOCIAL MEDIA

In this day and age, it's perfectly acceptable to use social media and the internet to archive your wedding ideas or memories. Using the space below, record details of your internet presence or take notes on who uploaded photos of your wedding so you can find them later.

WEDDING WEBSITE

URL

Login

Password

Description

FACEBOOK

Album Name

Hashtag

Notes

INSTAGRAM

Album Name

Hashtag

Notes

PINTEREST

Album Name ....

Notes ....

....

....

TWITTER

Album Name ....

Hashtag ....

Notes ....

....

....

PRO TIP: Establishing a hashtag for your wedding is a great way to allow your guests to document your big event in real time. It's also a handy way of creating a lasting digital keepsake for you!

RESOURCES

MAGAZINES

Brides Magazine (http://www.brides.com/)
Bridal Guide (http://www.bridalguide.com/)
Martha Stewart Weddings (http://www.marthastewartweddings.com/)

WEDDING BLOGS

Use the following for ideas, handy tips, and extra resources.
The Broke-Ass Bride (http://www.thebrokeassbride.com/):
    Wedding blog dedicated to tips for brides on a budget
Offbeat Bride (http://offbeatbride.com/):
    Wedding blog for quirky and fun wedding ideas
A Practical Wedding (http://apracticalwedding.com/)
    Wedding blog of down-to-earth wedding ideas

WEBSITES

MyRegistry (https://www.myregistry.com/wedding-registry.aspx):
    All-in-one site for wedding registries
Once Wed (http://www.oncewed.com/):
    Marketplace for second-hand bridal gowns and inspiration
    cache for DIY weddings

OTHER

....

....

....

....

NOTES

NOTES

NOTES

NOTES

NOTES

NOTES

NOTES